1 Inch Square by 14 Count Grid Sketchbook for Your Bad*ss Designs

Draw Accurately Sized
14 Count and 28 Over 2 Count
Needlework Charts and Patterns

The Snarky Cross Stabber

Arisa Williams

1 Inch Square by 14 Count Grid Sketchbook for Your Bad*ss Designs: Draw Accurately Sized 14 Count and 28 Over 2 Count Needlework Charts and Patterns

Series: DIY Design Supply Journals

ISBN: 9781091222335

Floss Chart

	Strand	Type	Number	Color	Alternate
	2	ANCHOR			

HAPPY
MOTHERS
DAY

HAPPY
MOTHERS
DAY

Floss Chart

	Strand	Type	Number	Color	Alternate

Floss Chart

	Strand	Type	Number	Color	Alternate

Floss Chart

	Strand	Type	Number	Color	Alternate

Floss Chart

	Strand	Type	Number	Color	Alternate

Floss Chart

	Strand	Type	Number	Color	Alternate

Floss Chart

	Strand	Type	Number	Color	Alternate

Floss Chart

	Strand	Type	Number	Color	Alternate

Floss Chart

	Strand	Type	Number	Color	Alternate

Floss Chart

	Strand	Type	Number	Color	Alternate

Floss Chart

	Strand	Type	Number	Color	Alternate

Floss Chart

	Strand	Type	Number	Color	Alternate

Floss Chart

	Strand	Type	Number	Color	Alternate

Floss Chart

	Strand	Type	Number	Color	Alternate

Floss Chart

	Strand	Type	Number	Color	Alternate

Floss Chart

	Strand	Type	Number	Color	Alternate

Floss Chart

	Strand	Type	Number	Color	Alternate

Floss Chart

	Strand	Type	Number	Color	Alternate

Floss Chart

	Strand	Type	Number	Color	Alternate

Floss Chart

	Strand	Type	Number	Color	Alternate

Floss Chart

	Strand	Type	Number	Color	Alternate

Floss Chart

	Strand	Type	Number	Color	Alternate

Floss Chart

	Strand	Type	Number	Color	Alternate

Floss Chart

	Strand	Type	Number	Color	Alternate

Floss Chart

	Strand	Type	Number	Color	Alternate

Floss Chart

	Strand	Type	Number	Color	Alternate

Floss Chart

	Strand	Type	Number	Color	Alternate

Floss Chart

	Strand	Type	Number	Color	Alternate

Floss Chart

	Strand	Type	Number	Color	Alternate

Floss Chart

	Strand	Type	Number	Color	Alternate

Floss Chart

	Strand	Type	Number	Color	Alternate

Floss Chart

	Strand	Type	Number	Color	Alternate

Floss Chart

	Strand	Type	Number	Color	Alternate

Floss Chart

	Strand	Type	Number	Color	Alternate

Floss Chart

	Strand	Type	Number	Color	Alternate

Floss Chart

	Strand	Type	Number	Color	Alternate

Floss Chart

	Strand	Type	Number	Color	Alternate

Floss Chart

	Strand	Type	Number	Color	Alternate

Floss Chart

	Strand	Type	Number	Color	Alternate

Floss Chart

	Strand	Type	Number	Color	Alternate

Floss Chart

	Strand	Type	Number	Color	Alternate

Floss Chart

	Strand	Type	Number	Color	Alternate

Floss Chart

	Strand	Type	Number	Color	Alternate

Floss Chart

	Strand	Type	Number	Color	Alternate

Floss Chart

	Strand	Type	Number	Color	Alternate

Floss Chart

	Strand	Type	Number	Color	Alternate

Floss Chart

	Strand	Type	Number	Color	Alternate

Floss Chart

	Strand	Type	Number	Color	Alternate

Floss Chart

	Strand	Type	Number	Color	Alternate

Floss Chart

	Strand	Type	Number	Color	Alternate

Floss Chart

	Strand	Type	Number	Color	Alternate

Floss Chart

	Strand	Type	Number	Color	Alternate

Floss Chart

	Strand	Type	Number	Color	Alternate

Floss Chart

	Strand	Type	Number	Color	Alternate

Floss Chart

	Strand	Type	Number	Color	Alternate

Floss Chart

	Strand	Type	Number	Color	Alternate

Floss Chart

	Strand	Type	Number	Color	Alternate

Floss Chart

	Strand	Type	Number	Color	Alternate

Floss Chart

	Strand	Type	Number	Color	Alternate

Floss Chart

	Strand	Type	Number	Color	Alternate

About The Snarky Cross Stabber

Arisa Williams of The Snarky Cross Stabber creates specialized sketchbooks for needlework and fiber arts. Find her Bad*ss chart and pattern aides on Amazon.

Series: DIY Design Supply Journals

10-Square Grid Sketchbook for Your Bad*ss Designs: Draw Your Own Subversive Needlework Charts and Patterns

1 Inch Square by 12 Count Grid Sketchbook for Your Bad*ss Designs: Draw Accurately Sized 12 Count and 24 on 2 Count Needlework Charts and Patterns

1 Inch Square by 14 Count Grid Sketchbook for Your Bad*ss Designs: Draw Accurately Sized 14 Count and 28 Over 2 Count Needlework Charts and Patterns

1 Inch Square by 16 Count Grid Sketchbook for Your Bad*ss Designs: Draw Accurately Sized 16 Count and 32 Over 2 Count Needlework Charts and Patterns

1 Inch Square by 18 Count Grid Sketchbook for Your Bad*ss Designs: Draw Accurately Sized 18 Count and 36 Over 2 Count Needlework Charts and Patterns

Printed in Great Britain
by Amazon

36307879R00072